WATCHERS OF
THE SEVEN SPHERES

BY

H. K. CHALLONER

With an Introduction by
THE AUTHOR OF " THE INITIATE," ETC.

With eight colour plates

LONDON
GEORGE ROUTLEDGE & SONS, LTD.
BROADWAY HOUSE, CARTER LANE, E.C.4
1933

Master Hilarian showing himself in Deva form.

PRINTED IN GREAT BRITAIN BY HEADLEY BROTHERS
109 KINGSWAY, LONDON, W.C.2 ; AND ASHFORD, KENT

DEDICATED WITH GRATITUDE

AND DEVOTION TO

THE MASTER HILARION

I wish to express my great indebtedness
to David Anrias and to Rose and
Cyril Scott for the help and the
encouragement they have given
to me in all my work

WATCHERS OF THE SEVEN SPHERES

INTRODUCTION

BY

THE AUTHOR OF *The Initiate*, ETC.

THE Christians have always believed in incorporeal beings such as angels, the Hindu Yogis and mystic in devas, and the Celts in fairies, gnomes and a multitude of other nature-spirits. With the Yogi, however, the term deva is a generic one, comprehending hosts of non-physical entities ranging from the smallest elf to Cosmic Beings of inconceivable grandeur. Have these entities any real existence, or are they merely products of the imagination or figures in systems of religio-philosophy? The materialist answers both the latter questions with an emphatic yes. Not so the trained Initiate in Esoteric Science, whose clairvoyant faculties have been directed towards the subtler manifestations of Nature. Not so even the naturally clairvoyant Scot or Irishman who, possessing what is termed " second sight", can behold the fairies at play, the undines sporting in the water-falls, the salamanders in the hearth-fire, the sylphs moulding the clouds into ever-changing shapes, or, in ominous contrast, the appearance of some unhappy elemental spirit auguring of evil to befall. For although lacking knowledge, he may be unaware of the fact, he is beholding some of the more primitive and more easily perceptible denizens of that great scheme of evolution which pursues its course concurrently with the human, and which is known in occult schools as the deva evolution or kingdom. This scheme is normally unperceived by humanity and in one sense apart from it, as the sea is apart from the land; yet far from exercising no influence whatever on us, its individual units are not only vitally involved in the ordering of our destiny, but are the wielders of mighty spiritual forces employed in the very building and sustaining of the Cosmos itself.

Indeed there are devas indigenous to every plane of consciousness. There are mountain-devas, devas who brood over volcanoes, devas who wield the lightning, devas connected with each and every religion, with each and every nation, with ceremonial, with art, music, literature and the drama, with science, with philanthropy and healing, in short with every branch of human endeavour as well as with every phase of Nature's activities. Thus when the materialist maintains that the processes of Nature are solely the outcome of mechanical forces, that hurricanes, for instance, are solely the result of great heat, he is possessed of but half the truth. And if he further maintains that chance is the sole cause why the lightning strikes and sets ablaze one house and not another, he is not even expressing half a truth. For the lightning, as conveyed in the following pages, is directed by the devas who in turn are under the commands of the great justice-dispensing Lords of Karma. Not by fortuitous chance does a man lose his property in that way, legally described as an " Act of God ", but as the result of some selfish act committed in the course of his long series of incarnations : probably some invocation of the fire-spirits for evil ends. And so when the ancient peoples believed in their gods of thunder, gods of the tempest, and so forth, they were not so superstitious and unenlightened as the later races in their arrogance and psychic blindness have imagined, since these natural forces are in truth ensouled by " gods " or rather devas, who are thus their personification and their directive agency.

The devas, in fact, may best be described as centres of force and intelligence who, under the direction of yet greater intelligences, carry out the functions of those particular offices to which they have been allocated. As already implied, it is the devas who inspire artists and art-movements, who inspire executants and especially composers,[1] who suggest to the poet combinations of beautiful words and melodious utterances, who endow the physician with " the touch that heals ", who vitalize and ensoul the higher types of all religious ceremonial. It is the devas who answer the prayers of the faithful and dispense comfort to those in need. Indeed they are ever ready to aid and give to Man according to the measure of his receptivity. But in order that he may the more receive, it is expedient that he should *know*. All forms of his creative activity inevitably attract the co-operation of the devas, but hitherto he has been unaware of this co-operation. Now the time has come when

[1] See *Music: Its Secret Influence throughout the Ages*. Cyril Scott. Rider & Co.

those who are the guardians of the race, and represent the inner spiritual government of the world, desire a closer contact between the members of the two evolutions. By degrees Man will acquire the power to work with the devas consciously, and to extend the field of knowledge along these lines this book has been written, as have some of its predecessors.[1] Yet even so " only a corner of the veil has been lifted ", and there is much esoteric information on the subject which can only be revealed to Initiates, who, working under the direct supervision of their own Masters,[2] can make these devic contacts with safety. The rationale of this process of safeguarding consists in consciously working with the Masters on a plane *above that on which co-operation with the devas is being attempted.*

Certain theosophical students have confined their attention almost entirely to those devas ensouling the ceremonies of the Christian religion, despite the fact that many signs are apparent showing that the fate of this religion is in the balance. For with each generation types of humanity change. Victorian veneration, whether for religion, elders or tradition, has passed away with the Victorian era itself. Modern clerics no longer command reverence from the critical and sophisticated youth of to-day. The priest is losing his hold, the inevitable Karmic retribution for insincerity, hypocrisy and the ceaseless intriguings of certain secret organizations.[3]

[1] See the works of C. W. Leadbeater and Geoffrey Hodgson.
[2] See page 61 (Mountain Spirit).
[3] See *The Vision of the Nazarene.* By the Author of *The Initiate.*

Thus the ceremonial devas who have played so important a part in the past, are being forced temporarily into the background, whilst those inspiring art and music are coming more to the fore.[1] The artist, the writer and the musician are to be greater channels for the devic activities of the comparatively near future. Religion, especially of the purely devotional type, is not the sole means by which humanity may evolve; it is only one of many, and not suited to every species of character. Religions wax and wane, since each successive religion is sponsored by the great Hierarchy in order to emphasize one particular aspect of Truth and not Truth in its entirety, which is beyond the grasp of the finite mind. Therefore will religions and kindred movements continue to be born and to die until this earth itself passes away.

Yet if this or that religion with its ritual, its priests and its prophets sinks into oblivion, not so Religion itself, that yearning in the heart of Man for the understanding of and union with the Divine. Thus we have read of a vision of the future given to a noted modern seer[2] foreshadowing several specialized forms of religious ceremonies in which *the devas themselves will act as hierophants*, those who participate having become sufficiently clairvoyant to perceive and co-operate with them. Needless to say, this is but one example of the multifarious ways in which the union of the two forms of evolution will be utilized

[1] See *The Initiate in the Dark Cycle*, Chapter XIII.
[2] See *Man Whence, How and Whither*. C. W. Leadbeater.

by the Higher Ones for the expression of Beauty and Power.

.   .   .   .

And now finally a few explanatory words regarding the pupil who, under the guidance of the Adept known as Master Hilarion,[1] has with pen and brush made the daring attempt to portray some of the more exalted of the devas, and to transmit their thoughts to the world of men. I am requested, however, to say that only an inadequate impression of their superb and many-dimensional forms can be rendered. To depict these Beings exactly as they are is as impossible as to give an exact reproduction of an orchestral symphony on the pianoforte. Indeed for one thing their bodies comprise colours which do not come into the range of our limited physical perceptions, and for another like a kaleidoscope their forms and hues are constantly changing, and their auras expanding and contracting. Nevertheless the author is greatly to be complimented on the manner in which so difficult a task has been accomplished. Hitherto descriptions of the devas have appeared in theosophical literature, but to our knowledge no attempt has been made to paint them, so that in this respect the author stands as a courageous pioneer in an as yet unexplored country. Furthermore the book is a mine of poetical utterance and power of language, and even those who are by

[1] See *Through the Eyes of the Masters*. David Anrias.

temperament too sceptical to accept its claims, cannot fail to enjoy it as poetry alone.

For ourselves however we consider it yet another valuable contribution to the literature pertaining to the study of the unseen and its relation to the visible world.

WATCHERS OF THE SEVEN SPHERES

PISCES

I

THE LISTENERS

THE MASTER SPEAKS TO HIS PUPILS:

"He who desires to prove for himself the existence of the Shining Ones—angels, devas, gods, call them by whatsoever name you will—he who would hear the sweetness of their voices, see their bright shapes moving at their appointed tasks in perfect harmony with the Will which called them and all things forth into manifestation; he who would understand the laws of their being and would co-operate in their divine activities, let him learn to lift his consciousness above the conflicting and deceptive forms, changing illusions of stability, which torment the dweller in the world of sense. Let him seek that sphere where light and sound, in their infinitely changing shapes and patterns, reflect, as in a lake's still, midday surface, the flawless image of the Thought Divine.

"Here, unruffled by the capricious winds of emotion, he will perceive that which is hidden from those who as yet care not to know what is, what has been and what shall be.

Here he will learn to comprehend laws only revealed to those who, desiring truth above all else, focus their energies one-pointedly upon its attainment, and are willing to risk, to this end, the loss of all things that the world holds most dear.

" Yet do not think, O you who desire Sight, Vision and Knowledge, that easily—or in one life—can these be attained. Long and hard is the path; yet it must be trodden, not by a few alone but by the majority of men, if the human race is to reach those supreme heights of glory and achievement to which, in his noblest moments, man aspires.

" The age of such perfected and divine humanity, in harmony with itself and with all creation, is still infinitely remote; but that age will come, and it is for you, children of this present age of transition, to thrust open once again the doors to the Temple of Truth that the materialism of past centuries has kept so rigorously closed, and to take the first steps toward the light therein enshrined which will reveal to those who dare approach it how this union of men and of devas, without which a greater revelation of nature's laws will ever be impossible, may be more speedily brought about.

" But before this can be done it is essential that man should admit the existence of the Deva Hierarchy, those beings who are, in fact, the personification of all energy and of every element which enters into the manifestation of form. For Life, in its entirety, is deva essence. Man lives unceasingly in their emanations, although he knows it not; his work in the coming centuries is to discover how he may live consciously with them in knowledge and understanding.

" Once, long ago, men and devas did so dwell together in unity, but the memory of that age is obscured by the mists of legend and lingers alone in the myths and the fairy tales of the race.

"And as for centuries to mankind in general the deva kingdom has been invisible and even unknown, so save for the more enlightened who have become clairvoyant to the physical plane as some men have to the astral, the devas have ignored individual man, sensing him only as a cloud of light or a burst of music, a vibration harmonious or otherwise according to his nature.

" For to them all is vibration. It is their language, their key-note, the manifestation of God Himself. They dwell in a realm of ecstatic beauty and love, a realm of music visible in glittering, transient shapes, of colour audible in waves of exquisite sound; of perpetually whirling atoms of matter, changing, coalescing, separating in response to the propulsions of the creative energy which the devas themselves live solely to express.

" Thus only when man himself seeks to manifest the divine power of creation and, through an effort of will or by the force of love, gives forth a strong desire to build in mind or in matter, do they become aware of him. When this occurs those devas attuned to whatever note he sounds are drawn irresistibly towards him and remain caught within the vortex of energy he has generated, continuing to play their vitalizing force upon it until the primary impulse fades or the form is completed.

" It follows then, that it is for man consciously to approach the devas, if he desires to be instrumental in

bringing about this new contact between the two
kingdoms and to work with the divine plan for the
evolution of the coming race.

" For at the inception of every new age in the history
of mankind Those who control and guide the government
of the inner worlds inaugurate some special line of
development whereby all beings will be enabled to acquire
new powers which will give them insight into the as yet
unrevealed aspects of the One Truth.

" To this end a great outpouring of spiritual energy
is vouchsafed to stimulate the higher bodies of those who
are capable of response ; and so it is that at this present
time new initiations are even now being evolved under
the Great One, our Lord, the Mahachohan, Who in His
mighty wisdom directs all lines of activity upon the earth.
Those who are capable of taking these initiations will have
for their especial work to open men's eyes to the wonders
of the deva kingdom and to hasten the day of co-operation
between the twain.   For, as the number of men who
learn to speak with the language of the gods increases, so
members of the deva hierarchy will come through them
more clearly to apprehend the nature of form manifesting
in the denser vibrations ; and this increased understanding
will enable them to take a still more active and intelligent
part in man's struggle to synthesize his bodies and to help
him in all his activities.   Many, indeed, through the
close sympathy which will in time develop between
individual members of the two kingdoms, will be drawn
—as a few have been in the past—into the human kingdom
and take human bodies.

" Already, although the new race is but in its inception,
great waves of force, more especially from the Sign

Aquarius, which will have a very important influence on the new race type, have been released to play upon the earth. The effect of this influx of energy will become more and more apparent as time goes on and new generations, attuned to its particular rate of vibration, are born. With this regenerating force, which will affect every part of man, even altering the order in which his life-centres are co-ordinated, will come, inevitably, hosts of Aquarian devas ; for each deva kingdom is affiliated with a particular type of force emanating from one of the Zodiacal signs.

" These devas and many more from Sagittarius and other Signs closely connected with the building and preparing of the races of the future, will be the divine messengers, pouring into the hearts and minds of men strange desires, thoughts, hopes and aspirations.

" Their work can already be discerned. The search for new forms of self-expression in art and in life ; the discoveries in the realms of science and in psychology ; the increasing effort man is making to lift the veil from the unseen worlds and to apprehend truth with fourth dimensional vision ; all these are but the reflection on earth of the activities upon the inner planes of these Builders of the New Age, who are ceaselessly impressing man's mind with the desire to acquire faculties he has not yet, but which it is their particular work to develop within him.

" In all ages throughout the whole of the evolution of humanity such work has been in progress, but each new age demands new methods ; and through a complete re-orientation of outlook alone can the modern man hope to bring about these changes which will mean so much to him.

" At this present time the seers of the race, responding to the particular influence of devas from the Sign Pisces which has now governed the world for many centuries, seek, as have done the mystics of the past, through devotion or through the power of will to still the mind and listen to inner voices. But the age of Pisces is waning; its devas are already being withdrawn before the invasion of those new forces of which I spoke, and man, swept forward upon these advancing waves of cosmic energy, is becoming ever more and more positive; he demands action, speed, mental efficiency in every branch of his activities. No longer content to listen to the voice of tradition or to the pronouncements of others, he wills to experiment—to become himself the KNOWER. Those, therefore, who would be the seers and spiritual leaders of this coming race will have, perforce, to learn how they may, through personal knowledge and control, attain to the understanding of and participation in the working of the laws of nature which this closer contact with the Deva Hierarchy will gradually reveal to those who are willing to study its mysteries.

" For man stands indeed upon the threshold of discoveries, of revelations, of the attainment of powers such as have not been known since the days of the Atlantean Race.

" And herein lies his danger. Unless, this time, he is morally strong enough to control these forces and develops that spirituality of outlook essential to all those who wield great power, once again he will be overwhelmed; once again he will be swept to destruction by the very forces which are designed to be his benefactors.

" It is from this, the fell fruit of his own ignorance and pride, that we seek to protect him ; and it is to this end that I desire to reveal to you some of the difficulties which must be faced and overcome if man is to learn to contact the devas with impunity.

" For again I would stress that the devas respond to the creative vibration a man gives forth, to the Note of Will or of Love or of Activity that he sounds upon the aeolian harp of the inner worlds. As his motives are, so will his note manifest there, either in harmony or in discord ; in floods of exquisite colour or suffused with the crude shades of his own aura—and according to this Note will be the type of devas he attracts to himself.

" And herein lies the key to the dangers which attend this fusion of the human and deva lines of evolution ; for although both are united in aim and are proceeding towards one goal, their natures are utterly unlike. The devas are not possessed, as is man, of a sense which differentiates between right and wrong ; therefore, because of their very nature, void of error, or of the possibility thereof, those who function on the lower planes of the Astral and Etheric can be used by man for good or for ill.

" Only those possessed of a clear understanding of the fundamental laws of nature can, therefore, hope to invoke the devas with safety. For if a man attempt so to do before he has learned a great measure of control over his emotional and mental bodies, under the tremendous outpouring of force which his invocation will draw upon him he may easily be overpowered and driven eventually to what men, in their ignorance, mis-name madness.

" This is one of the most common causes of the tragedy of so many of those sensitive and gifted ones who possess some of the powers of genius, but lack its higher attributes. With mighty, one-pointed will the man invokes the creative energies ; the devas rush in ; he opens himself to them promiscuously, to the lowest as to the highest, knowing not how to discriminate between them. For a while he sees through devic eyes, hears through their immortal ears, is the recipient of some little of their knowledge, becomes forgetful of all the limitations of time and the conventional laws of less gifted men. But when the impulse slackens and the devic forces withdraw, he finds himself mentally and emotionally an empty, abandoned shell, yet still possessed of a residue of the creative energy uncorrelated within him. He who, even if unconsciously, has been trained in control, would know by instinct how to raise this surplus force from the solar plexus—through which most of the devic energy is poured —to the higher centres, but the average man will be helpless and allow the force to flood his lower centres, thus causing terrible unbalance, emotional stress and often acute sexual disturbance.

" This type of man lives ever in a world of extremes, of sudden ecstasy, of misery and despair. If then he be by nature weak, feeling himself abandoned by the stimulating influences which give him joy, he will begin to invoke those lower elemental entities who cannot function in the higher centres, and will often by them be driven to excess and degradation.

" Equally, should any seek to use the devas with deliberate intent for selfish or destructive purpose, let him beware ! Eventually the result will be disaster ; for the note he sounds will be a false one, setting up a dissonance with the creative note of the divine Will ; upon this discord the deva essence will vibrate with greater and greater momentum until the man can no longer control it ; gradually the increasing vibration will begin to disintegrate his bodies until finally they will be destroyed by paralysis, apoplexy, or by the slower process of some cancerous disease. Finally—I say : this may not happen in one life. Be it known to you that those who in Atlantis and even in later times thus trafficked with the devas, have been forced to re-incarnate with the discord which they themselves created sounding still within them ; vibrating ever upon their etheric matter it causes ill-health, disease or death according to its strength and their own weakness. It must eventually be transmuted by the man himself into harmony through service and through love ; and he is ready to be ' cured ' only when his note peals forth once more in unison.

" Nor have these powers been perverted to base usage in the past alone ; still in some Indian cults, and in the depraved rites of savages, who have retained half-forgotten fragments of the old Mysteries, the lower elemental forms are called into activity by the rhythmic beat of drums and the shrill, reiterated notes of primitive instruments. Yet worse, by far, is their invocation through the ceremonial rites and secret magic of certain religious organizations who seek, by means of devic energy, to enslave their adherents to their will by playing upon their uncontrolled emotions and ignorant fears. To these, the more enlightened, will come retribution, terrible and swift, when the hour strikes for the new outpouring of Love to flood the world with light and to open blinded eyes.

" Yet only the lower devas can be thus used for personal ends ; those who are highly evolved, who have advanced as far along their line as pupils of the Masters have done on earth, would never respond to any vibration save that vitalized by pure love and desire to serve the divine ends. Nor would their note be revealed to any worker on the Left Hand Path, as it is only to those who have taken deva initiations that the secrets are unveiled, and these can only be taken on the inner planes when the man is ready to serve and to obey—never before.

" Therefore again I say unto you, let none attempt these contacts until he has proved himself fitted so to do. I may seem, perhaps, to repeat this particular warning too persistently, but I know full well how prone are men to ignore or immediately to forget any particular aspect of truth which they do not wish to admit, or to which some secret part of them is in resistance. But this aspect of which I speak cannot with impunity be ignored or forgotten, and for that reason alone I stress it, as do the devas themselves.

" Remember therefore my words and meditate thereon.

" Understanding and control of the bodies is the road; love and service the bridge which leads across the gulf separating the two Kingdoms still.

" For love is the vibration to which all nature responds; it is the key-note of creation. To every outpouring of selfless love the devas answer joyfully, entering the man who loves, increasing his power with their own. All men may worship, may invoke these messengers of the divine regenerative power, in safety ; no harm can come to him who strives to find the perfect rhythm within himself, who desires to pour himself out in adoration and in service ; for by this very act he contacts the devas through the God within his own heart Who cannot but sound their note aright, since He is one with them, another spark from the One Flame.

" Therefore that man who feels burning within himself an ardent desire to work henceforth towards this glorious goal of union between devas and men, let him go forward, fearing nothing, yet realizing to the full the magnitude of his task.

" For first of all he must face HIMSELF ; he must learn to know the man he is and to see whether indeed he is ready to undertake this work which requires specific qualities of mind, body and spirit. To this end he would do well to gaze at that image of his true self, created by him in past lives, which is ever revealed by the position of the planets and conjunctions of the luminaries at birth. If, reading aright their secret symbols, he see that he is not yet fitted for this work, let him not despair. He has the power to build for himself through meditation and a continual striving toward spiritual growth, bodies which, in his next life, will enable him to do all that he desires. But if the stars should point him the way, in this life, to achievement, then must he begin his training by learning first to control all selfish longing for objects of sense ; he must desire truth, knowledge, wisdom, not for himself, but that he may lay them at the feet of his fellow men; he must learn indifference to disaster, defeat, aye, even to death. He

must be willing to allow himself to be segregated from
the group-mind of those men who still function collec-
tively, and to stand with boldness upon his chosen path,
ready to act, and if that action be mistaken, to pay the
price. He must give years to strenuous training, as
would an athlete who trains for the course ; he must have
patience infinite, never seeking to rouse before their time
those faculties which lie dormant in every man, but
cannot safely be stirred to action until the man is strong
enough to bear the responsibility which their awakening
will entail. He must learn, having stilled the emotions,
killed out desire and slain ambition, to function upon
that plane where Truth may be apprehended, the plane
of Intuition, where the soul can touch its divine Source.

" Then to him will the Spirits of the Air, the Fire,
the Water and the Earth open wide the doors of their
Kingdoms.

" Go then all you whose eyes are turned towards this
goal, seek now to lift your consciousness into the bright
heart of that Brotherhood who, in the long course of
their evolution have become the messengers of the Adepts
and have grown to apprehend man through the minds of
those who exist only to serve his needs.

" Some have been bidden to contact you and to
co-operate in this work for which you have been prepared.

" Vibrate then to their note ; keep your mind clear
as a pure crystal, unclouded by any mists of personal
emotion or desire.

" Be still. Listen. Then will they draw near ; then
will they speak. They will unite themselves with you
and through you they will answer to the note which man,
in his present need has sounded forth."

ARIES

II

THE SOLAR DEVA

I am a Ray from our Lord,
The Lord of Light.
He is the Fire Creative;
He is one with the Hidden Word
Which, thrilling through the Cosmos,
Maketh itself manifest
In the mighty Builders
Whose reflections
Am I.

I am the Intermediary;
Through me in my multitudinous forms
Pulseth for ever
The urge, which is Life.

I am the Response;
In me sounds the Note
Which calls to the Shining Ones,
The atoms of energy,
Whirling, propelling them
Into the mystic danse
Which becometh a planet, a star,
A man—or a clod of earth.

I am the Destroyer;
When the Note changeth,
Into myself,

Into the vortex of my being,
I withdraw.
Slowly the rhythm grows fainter;
The atoms disintegrate;
The impulsions pass onward
Into another womb.
One form is no more;
Another cometh to birth.

I am limitless;
For I vibrate to the pulse
Of That which hath no limitation.
I obey.
I thrill to the bliss
Of That which, in harmony,
Worketh ever towards perfection
Through my Lord, the Hidden, the mysterious SUN.
I am the focus for That
Which is nameless and unconditioned.
I expand—I contract.
I am conscious in the infinitesimal life of the earth's core;
I rejoice with the joy of the blossom opening to the
    light;
I am the song of the Heavenly Ones, the Note of creation;
From whatsoever plane I receive in my being
The thrill of harmony, of creative desire—of love,
To that I respond—to that call I come;
Swifter than thought I come;
Yea, at the thought I am there;
For I am that.

O Thou Effulgent Life,
Love manifested forth
Into man's darkness,
I, flame of Thy Flame,
Dwell in Thy Heart of Light.
At Thy command I speed
Blazing with triple fires
Into the hearts of those who can invoke Thy Power.

As yet only few have learnt
To gaze without flinching into Thy dread face ;
And unto them,
In the deep silence of the Fire
Which burneth ever without heat
Thy voice is heard.
To these, the Enlightened Ones, is given
Power to reflect something of what they see
Into the more receptive minds among the sons of men,
That man thus may glimpse the shadow of Thy glory
Mercifully tempered to his weakness,
And vision faintly That of which he is a part.
'Tis we—'tis we—glad spirits, sons of the Flame, are
      used
To draw man unto Thee, his Source ;
'Tis we who inspire in him love and desire
For Thee, Light of his being ;
And through Thy pure essence,
Thy spiritual glory
We seek to evolve from the youth of the world
A new race to serve Thee,
Who, lit by Thy Light and inspired by Thy Breath,
May draw from Thy Being powers of mind, spirit and
      body.
This is the work for which we were created—
The evolution of form, the releasing of spirit
From bondage ; the fusing of each flame with its primal
      fire,
The Spiritual Sun, the Logos, our Lord !
O Life of our Life,
O Heart of Pure Fire,
We worship Thee, we live to obey Thee
Who, in Thy wisdom stupendous
Controlleth Thy Seven Sons,
The Lords of the Planets.
They, stretching Their hands toward Thee,
Invoking Thy wisdom, dwell within Thy light.
Thou dost direct their impulsions,
Their courses, their wills ;

Preventing the conflict of their mighty forces
Which stream ever outward
Affecting each other, as man's every action
For good or for ill, affects the lives of his brothers.
Thou blendest their notes, interweaving their harmonies
Into new forms;
Renewing their life and the lives of all beings
Who are part of their substance,
Forever evolving toward that perfection,
The form archetypal,
Revealed unto Thee through divine Ideation.
For behold, even Thou, Solar Logos, our Lord,
Even Thou bendest Thy shining head to the will of
     Another,
Knowing Thyself but a part of a mightier Scheme,
Of which He, the Unknown One, the Centre,
Is no more than the servant of ONE great beyond thought,
WHO again stretches upward, growing, evolving
In knowledge and wisdom,
Towards THAT which is Nameless,
Which is DARKNESS and SILENCE.

     .   .   .   .

O man, who at last, once more
Yearns towards knowledge;
We see you—we hear you,
Struggling upward—awakening; casting off the fetters
     of custom.
Naked and strong as the Greeks, the Egyptians,
Worshippers of the Sun,
Who drew life from His rays and rejoiced in His light,
Raise up your hearts again to the Lord of your being!
For growth, healing, enlightenment send forth supplica-
     tion!
Prepare to receive the powers which He bringeth
Unto His votaries:
The strong form perfected—temple fitted for light;
The mind clear and lucid;
And greatest of all, the spirit untrammelled
That leapeth to heights divine,

That uniteth itself with the rays of the planets,
That defieth destruction ;
That entereth fearless
Within the dread Portals,
Into the Primal Fire,
Into the One Life,
Into the Heart of the Sun.

TAURUS

III

THE EARTH SPIRIT

A strange vibration pulses through my being;
I am aware of one working upon my rays
Who, through power and through devotion
Unites himself with the creative impulse
Which makes me what I am.
Now I direct my sight upon him;
I see the bright colours of his ringing Note,
Hear the pure rose and gold sounding within his heart,
Sweet strains of music which unite him
Unto us, whose focus is the growth and death
Of all things in the Second[1] Kingdom.
We approach him, I and my servants,
Nature sprites and gnomes,
Bright flower fairies and the dancing undines
That haunt the brooks,
All elementals that do work in earth, in water, sun or air.
Unto such men as this, our friend and our co-worker,
One with me and mine, Nature unveils her face.
At his vibration, strong, harmonious with her will,
Life stirs with eagerness in flower and plant.
To him we reveal our secret lore.
Love is the link between us,
For love is the primal impulse throughout the whole creation:
Desire for growth and union
With That which is greater than the separate self,
The mighty Being of which we and they

[1] The vegetable Kingdom.

35

And all that dwell on earth are cells of life :
The Planetary Logos,
Greater man and greater god than ever man can know.
He is our life ; we draw our life from Him.
Feeding upon His substance for our growth
We thus become a mystic centre wherein His will can mani-
     fest
And His mysterious purpose work
From highest unto lowest.
O, far into the earth my forces flow !
The metals, the rocks, stir in their motionless and dream-like
     state
As, uniting my consciousness with their indwelling life,
I re-charge their chemical atoms, separating the elements I
     need,
Drawing into myself a million tiny beings to work my will,
And within the unseen vortices of earth,
Stimulate growth where death seems lord of life.
I cause the water devas of the air to build their cloudy
     edifices,
And pour down their rain on thirsting fields.
'Tis I who call upon the sons of fire to send their vitalizing
     rays
That they may fecundate the waiting earth.
Within my being, all the lesser ones, my children,
Leap and play in mystic dance like motes in sunlight,
     dazzling through the air ;
Winged by the impulse of my will they fly to their
     appointed tasks.
All things in nature play their little part within the vaster
     plan.
The unseen insects creeping through the grass ;
The honey bee winging his heavy way through clover
     fields ;
The singing bird, building his tiny nest ;
The flowers, the plants, the trees—
Who love and live more consciously than all the other
     brethren of their kind—
Each builds and lives and dies according to the Law.

Guided by One mind, our lesser minds unite ;
Changing our forms, unceasingly we work in blissful
      ecstasy.
That which seems death to you, O man,
To us is perfect rhythm, a harmony of millions of voices
Sweeping throughout the spheres in outpourings of joy.
Nowhere is there cessation of that song called Life.
All life createth life.
The great wheels turn in cyclic motion
Bearing all things toward one consummation ;
But the one discord is the voice of man
Who, in his ignorance, still strives to work apart.
Ah, if he knew his power ! If he but understood
How, because of him, the harmony remaineth incomplete,
How he alone preventeth the upward surge of evolution !
Yet already in the dim recesses of his perturbèd mind,
Like a small seed within which the life force striveth
Through its dark prison of earth toward the light,
The spirit urgeth him to seek release,
Driving him relentlessly ever toward the quest for Truth.
Yea, I perceive even now his Note vibrating into my
      centres
With a cry for union, for an expression of life,
Which only we can give.
Let it but grow stronger until I and mine
Are enabled to respond in joyous rapture,
Then unto his dazzled sight will be revealed
The hidden beauties of the Second Kingdom.
He shall perceive us at our work in valley, wood and
      stream ;
Great shapes will fill his sky ; he will commune with every
      flower,
Aye, with each stone ; he shall hear the transcendent
      music of the stars ;
The sweeping winds, the glittering waters will reveal
      their souls and speak with him ;
To him will come the birds—all the wild things, savage
      and shy alike
Will seek him out and walk beside him unafraid.

Then will he be taught to blend his energies with ours
      and work with us;
Then will he realize all Kingdoms are his own
When he hath learnt to sound their Note aright,
Give forth the Words of Power:
Love—Service—
Unity of Purpose
With That which
We serve.

IV

THE BUILDER OF FORM

A call resounds. Clear as a silver bell
It vibrates throughout the spheres
In quivering waves of light.
The Karmic hour, inevitable, strikes.
The impulse to create, stirs, strives, attracts.
From out the Holy Place,
The Secret Place
Where dwell the Mighty Ones Who mete out justice to
    each living thing,
Without Whose sanction nought may come to birth,
Sanction is given.
At the Word,
Magnetic waves surge forth to their appointed task.
We come—Builders of Form, we come!
Thought hath compelled us.
To that place we speed whence like hath called to like.
Invoke us and we stand ready to do thy will;
We cannot fail to answer to the Note which bids us serve.

.   .   .   .

Behold me, I am here!
I am the matrix.
Within my mind the imaged thought shines clear;
Through me its life must come.
Whatever be the dream that glows in the creator's mind
That will I seek to build
So long as the clear thought reflects itself in me, unwaver-
    ing and unchanged.

Through every channel the great power which I may use
Flows in.
So much—no more.
Be it a child, a flood of music, an empire or a song that is
   conceived on earth,
The Law remains : so much force and no more.
So much ! I feel the waves
Pulsing and playing in my golden heart.
A myriad lives are drawn into my life ;
Mine is their joy.
Within my womb they build, they coalesce.
Potent with their new life I too expand.
I sweep their forces on in patterns and shapes of colour
   and of sound.
The clear form grows.
The power is converging now with ever increasing might
Towards its focus on the physical plane.
The centres rotate in unison ;
The vortex glows.
Into the heart of him whose strong desire
Conjured me forth with all the powers I wield,
The energies, the fiery atoms drive
Until the work is done.
The artist, the musician, he who seeks to trap a dream
   with words,
Actors, inventors, all those in whom the creative impulse
   stirs,
Although they do not know my form,
Recognize and acclaim me when my emanations flow into
   their minds.
Their blood runs swifter ; joy leaps within their hearts.
They are themselves, yet mightier than themselves
For they are me.
Magnified, transfigured, glorified, they become in the
   divine moment of creative energy
One with all lives in me, and with that greater Life
Of which I am th' embodiment.
In me It manifests to them and inspiration pours into the
   mould of form.

I am the spirit of re-birth.
Through me the germs of life are coalesced
Within the Mother's womb
When the configurations of the stars propitious stand.
Through my life pass the elements of this new life ;
The astral currents bring to me forms from the past,
Results of causes which, generated by acts in other lives,
Until their Note sounds, sleep as if forgot.
A thousand elements co-operate.
The child's egoic form watches and aids through me,
Already tied to its inevitable fate
By thread as fine as silver spiders' web, yet strong as steel.
We draw the force from those we may.
From parents take etheric matter ; from all nature's
 kingdoms, particles of life,
Little or much according to the merits of the soul which
 seeks new birth.
And as the work goes on,
Within the hidden matrix of my heart glows the child's
 form—a jewel, a bud of light.

I am the Virgin Mother ; the spirit of the primaeval
 ocean
Whence all things were conceived and all forms drawn
 anew.
With me the healers come, sons of violet etheric waves
Who guide and inspire the minds of those who seek to
 understand and cure
The manifold ills of men ;
For ours is the task to build humanity ever anew,
Leading it on from strength to strength, towards its full
 fruition,
The apex of its glory, the mighty Race to be, who con-
 sciously
Will see us, know us, work as now we work
In harmony with the ¹Lipika Lords, the Adepts, the
 whole vast scheme

¹ Lords of Karma.

Which urges all manifested life towards perfected
      harmony.
O you, the wise, co-operate with me !
Hold your bright forms inviolate ;
Pour forth your love, your pure desire to us,
And we will quicken it and vitalize
With fire and water, with the elements of air and
      earth,
The Sacred Four :
Pure fire, the mental flame, essence of life ;
Water, the symbol of the astral powers, illusory, the doom
      of men's desires,
Already in all lower forms fatally interwoven ;
Air, the swift, rushing messengers who come as winds to
      purify the form ;
And earth, the only part man knows as yet, which binds
      him still a helpless prisoner.

Behold me then—the Messenger, glowing with love !
Evoke me—I reply.
Yet be thou warned, O man, who in thy pride and
      strength,
Thinketh perchance to use powers and elements thou
      canst not yet control.
I am the agent of the Karmic Law.
To him who seeketh my rich gifts for dark forbidden
      purpose ;
To him who would create distorted shapes and crude
      disharmonies,
Evil that will curse the lives of men,
My powers indeed will come, since he hath free-will to
      choose,
But with them comes also his retribution, for they will
      be his doom.
'Twere better he had been born as his fellow men,
Blind, deaf and dumb to these great potencies which lie
      within man's jurisdiction ;
For he who useth Force against the Law
By Force will be destroyed.

But those who will learn, who even now are learning, how
      to speak
Our language, how to hear the harmonies we give forth,
To work with us, and with us strive to obey the Will
      Divine,
Them shall the Devas gladly serve.
They shall become as we;
To them shall Truth unveil her face;
They shall be free
To wield our powers,
And sound the Note of Form.

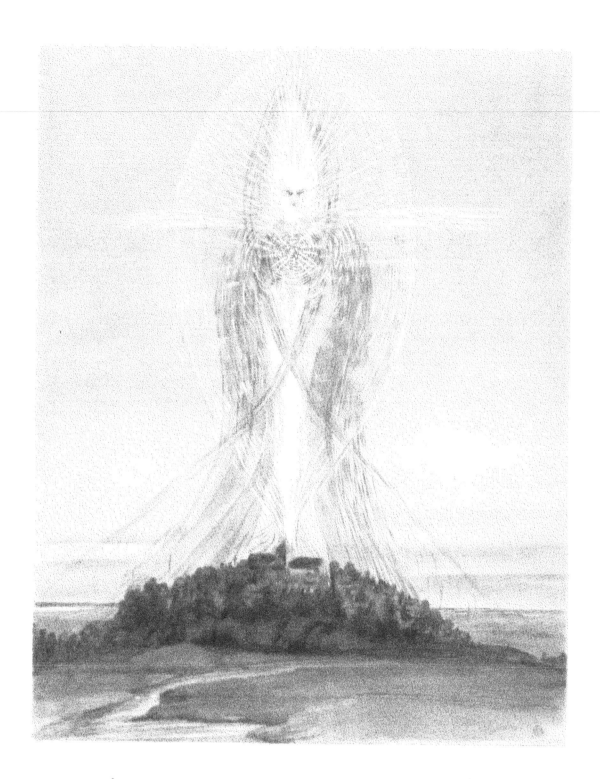

CANCER

V

THE DEVAS OF CEREMONIAL

We brood, we watch, we wait.
From man's primaeval, blind desire for union with That
    from which he came
Were we created.
We will be till that desire is consummated,
And we too, with man, return into the glory whence all
    things emerged.

There is no place, however low and humble, consecrated
    by the use of prayer and praise
Unblessed by one of our great Brotherhood,
And by those mightier ones, Adepts in love, who are our
    Lords.
Our strength, our beauty and our power to bless
Grow by the force which emanates from priest and
    worshipper;
According to its measure we are enabled thus
To shower our benedictions forth.
When instrument and voice unite in praise and love and
    worship,
And lifted on wings of pure one-pointed will flood us
    with power and glory,
Then we expand and glow.
Bright rays leap from our eyes; the jewel heart within
    focusseth light,
The mystic Rose unfolds.
The Word goes forth; flashing from East and West

45

Our Brethren come to join their strength with ours
And far and wide peace and rejoicing bless the hearts of
  men.
Magic our nature is ; magic of ritual, music and word
  conjured us once
To stimulate and influence the minds of those
Who held the secret and could sound the Note
Of sacred invocation.
But now no more the mystic harmonies of sound rever-
  berate through the triple worlds.
Now no more pure waves of light, fair colours, elemental
  shapes
Of beauty rise from temple and from grove.
That age is past.
Now the mumbling priest, the scanty worshippers
Who cling to old traditions and whose minds like wanton
  breezes
Cannot retain a thought beyond the moment ;
The sad, discordant jingle of faint sound, the words,
  devoid of knowledge as of sense,
Have not the power to call our glory down.
Faintly our forms appear ; dimmed are our pristine rays
As shadows seen in some cracked, ancient glass.
How can we then still generate the powers which stir the
  heart,
And raise man's consciousness to states of ecstasy,
Whence wisdom falls like dew upon his arid mind, and he
  beholds
His Lord and ours—supreme ?
Man hath forgot and turned himself away,
For those who have been the guardians of the Sacred Lore
Have failed him and poisoned the bright wells at which
  he drank ;
And through the growing faculties of his awakening mind
He hath outstripped them.
No longer will he walk the mystic path whereon he
  believes himself to have been deceived ;
No longer doth he hope to find the truth he seeks through
  ceremonial rites.

Those ancient sacraments of unsurpassèd beauty,
The united voice and act of worshippers, the rhythmic
    movement,
This magic which brought us down to unite our con-
    sciousness with that of the participants,
And give them super-terrestrial vision,
This hath now become a legend—an idle poet's dream ;
For from the heart of ceremonial the holy mysteries have
    been withdrawn,
And now being empty can no more answer man's need,
    since it doth fail to stir his senses
Or his mind, tuned to another key.
O man, knowing no other source at which to slake your
    raging thirst for Truth
Ye wander down strange ways, seeking your gods on earth,
And finding nought but broken images !
Yet ye have willed to walk alone,
And lonely, stumble through th' encompassing dark,
Unlit by those clear stars which once gave life to all your
    works.
So shall it be while still ye refuse to pass
The dread portals of ancient mysteries.
Now your idle feet sound hollowly on temple floors
    deserted
Where in ancient days the power of God took form
And priest initiates wrought what would to you seem
    miracles.
So ignorant ye have become, ye can no more distinguish
    Error from Truth ;
Forfeited are your powers—and it is well.
Not yet are ye ripe for the new dawn of knowledge ;
Ye have too much to learn.
Now we can give you nought but guardianship and pity ;
We can only meet the less with less.
Nothing can come from nothing.
When once again man learns his innate need
And cries to be shown the way of wisdom,
When he seeks to unite himself with us
Through service, devotion and the rites of love ;

When from the earth's aura are effused the rays of roseate
     harmony,
Where now the scarlet blaze of conflict glows,
Then to man's call the Great Ones will reply ;
Then will descend on earth an impulse new ;
Wise teachers will return to guide the Race and to unveil
Another aspect of the face of Truth,
Founding great schools where mysteries will be revealed
And Nature's powers disclosed to those
Who can be brave, pure, silent and controlled.
Then to meet the new needs will be evolved new forms
     of worship ;
New words of Power to take the place of those
Which have been desecrated in usage base by the deluded
     men
Who work against the Law.
When once again the celestial waves of sound rise up
     to us from earth,
Calling us down in glory and in might,
Then in that day we will descend with power,
Our pure Ray shining forth anew in all its pristine beauty,
In symphonies of colour, light and sound.
Then, heralded by us, will return in majesty,
The mighty Lord of Love,
Who cometh only when through love and ardent desire
     for growth,
Man calleth Him down into the place prepared where He
     can manifest.
In your own hands, O man, is your own fate.
Time for us is not.
Until that day dawn when, strong and wise,
Ye understand yourselves and use aright your own glorious
     potentialities,
We, your servants, brothers, lords,
We brood—we watch—we wait.

LEO

VI

THE NATIONAL DEVA

I am the great Guardian;
I unite and coalesce within my being the hopes and aspira-
tions
Generated by that chosen group of men I live to serve.
I am the embodiment of the national thought,
The people's tendencies, their dreams, their aspirations,
The invisible symbol of their collective life,
The Form they have themselves, through their own
thoughts, evolved.
I stand perpetually brooding o'er their land;
I change with their continual changing;
I evolve with them.
To me is given power to mitigate through transmutation
Their errors, in accordance with the will for good inherent
in them.
I am their pride of Race.
I come to birth at the first national act,
And from that moment evermore I work upon their
hidden centres,
Leading them on and upward.
At the beginning, when, like a tender child
The Nation stumbles, striving toward control, unity of
will and purpose,
I focus its aspirations in mine own clear heart, stimulat-
ing its self-consciousness,
Filling it with desire for achievement and to shine above its
fellows;

I segregate it, turning it inward upon itself ;
Feed it with religions proper to its spiritual growth ;
I give it lines of Kings, that it may learn to idealize itself
  in them ;
I give it lords of war and peace, leaders and teachers to
  intensify
Its energies within the triple worlds of matter, mind and
  spirit.
Thus I do lead its childish steps towards maturity.
Later when it hath grown and the urge for expansion,
  prowess and adventure stirs within,
Then do I fire the imaginations of its poets with a thousand
  chimeras of glory,
And lead the Nation forth to where its capacities
May find expression and a wider scope.
Then it doth break its childhood bonds ; it sendeth its
  sons
To gather ideas, innovations, material benefits from others
  of its kind ;
To bear it children in far foreign lands, to conquer it
  fields
Where it may sow its seed, expand and grow.
Thus cometh it to its prime.
At last, flushed with achievement, proud, remote, apart,
It toucheth the danger line.
Strong, self-centred, in this its glorious maturity
It wills to stand supreme,
And draws into itself currents from every source, both
  good and ill.
It inciteth envy and fear.
Now it may become dazzled by desire for domination,
Enslaved by those vain ambitions which are conceived
  through pride ;
Men rise within its heart, inspired by the Dark Forces
  who
Seek ever to bring confusion to the earth.
They urge the Nation forth on paths of useless conquest ;
They drive it to desire powers that it cannot hold and far
  less can control,

Stimulating all evil tendencies which it hath generated
    throughout its past.
Now is its hour of choice—its testing time.
For in it now, as in the body of man when once the apex
    of his life is passed,
The strength of youth is over, and the downward arc of
    form, of matter, hath begun,
Disintegration stirs.
Three pathways lie before it :
It may remain static, and tainted by inertia fall into quick
    decay ;
Or through pride and vain excess, through evil counsel,
    and a refusal
To see the truth, blindly it may rush on toward its
    inevitable doom,
Defeat, eclipse, annihilation.
But it can take the noblest path of all
And, turning once more its forces inward, revolving
Toward the things of mind and spirit, seek to perfect
    that work for which it was conceived ;
Then let it listen to the voice of those wise guardians of
    the Race,
The great men of its past, who bound to it by service and
    by love
Have become its Guides, its Masters and who, unknown,
    dwell hidden still in secret hiding-places.
Let it lay its bright sword aside, and strive with Them for
    peace ;
Inspired by Them it will raise its fiery potencies—the
    fruits of its endeavour on the long path of evolution —
Toward still greater heights of spiritual achievement and
    of glory
Before its day be done.
For pass it must ; the circle of birth and death is to be
    trod by all,
Man, Nation, World and System—that is the Law.
But O, my child, my offspring and creater both,
Be wise, refuse annihilation and the scorn which is given
    to the weak and fallen ;

Make thy decline a glory !
Let the powers of mind exalt it,
Let thine eyes shine with the light of youth eternal;
Unite thy hidden fires with those immortal Fires which burn
       in the mighty Beings,
Who brood over continents and oceans, who guide the
       policies of every race.
O, send me forth through the impulsion of thy enlight-
       ened mind
To unite myself with Them, The International Devas,
Who, to the world, are what I am to thee.
Then through their regenerating power new energy will
       re-vitalize
Thy dying form.
Thou wilt blaze up, thou wilt become a guiding star to
       Nations younger than thyself;
A torch by which men yet unborn will see the Path to
       wisdom.
Then through the impulse that thy transcendent power
       will give to life and form,
The greater world outside thyself will grow; taking its
       ideals of leadership
From thy renowned example.
Races to come will pour their blessing on thy name,
And thou wilt live again in them, through them receive
The transcendent gift of Immortality.

VII

THE INTERNATIONAL DEVA

We are the mighty Brotherhood of Peace and Evolution,
Ensoulèd first through the great mind of Him
Who is Himself the reflection of a higher will,
The Planetary Lord, the Silent Watcher;
He who hath sacrificed Himself that we and you, O men,
May be protected from those cosmic energies
Which, unchecked, would sweep us to destruction.
Remote we dwell, symbols of divine prescience—of
　　thought without emotion.
We discern the activities of earth as fluctuating currents
　　of light and sound;
As fine threads which we draw together and interweave
Into the sacred pattern we have been shown by Him
　　who guides us all.
We strive ever for unity, harmonizing the conflicting
　　vibrations which emanate
From each separate Nation according to its stage upon
　　the rungs of progress.
We work through those, our lesser Brethren, their guides,
Who, nearer to man, ensouled by his own thought, reveal
　　to us the trend of his development,
And act as intermediaries, drawing to him the energies
　　he needs from out our heart,
Leading him ever on to comprehend our will, our work,
　　our aims.
We it is who magnetize those centres where the sons of
　　men foregather

To evolve methods of international co-operation, to seek
     out paths of peace,
And to inaugurate reforms and laws to benefit mankind.
From the regenerating flame of their desire, we create the
     harmony necessary to their ends.
'Tis we who inspire the minds of their great men—bright
     lights shining through chaos—
Who, in response to our divine vibrations, invoke, through
     visions of progress, our power.
We endeavour to transmute the errors and the fears, the
     conflicts and confusions
Which arise through man's own blindness, into ultimate
     benefit, bringing swift retribution
That he may learn to associate Cause and Effect and
     recognize that evil and destruction breed nought
     but dissolution,
And love and harmony alone will lead him toward the
     perfect State
Of which his leaders and his seers dream.
Thus do we ever seek to draw all men into our own
     Brotherhood
Revealing to them the foolishness of separation and racial
     prejudice,
Necessary to the young but fatal curse on older nations
     who must learn to live in bonds of harmony or
     perish.
'Tis we, who, at this time, are striving to unite the spirit-
     ual wisdom of the East to those fine qualities of
     lower mind
The West hath now developed.
For until East and West can comprehend each others'
     thought,
Until the barriers of Race and Creed are down, and all
     men know that Truth is one ;
Until each country hath passed through the hot fires of
     experience and mastered its own control,
Finding its unity within and realizing that each one is
     part of all;
Until that time peace cannot reign on earth.

For discord lies, like to a snake, hidden within the tangled
  growth of separateness.
We are all One. Ye Nations of the earth, ye are the
  limbs, the organic forces, the dense body
Of the Planetary Lord.
Whilst ye remain in this fell state of discord and war
  perpetually the one against the other,
Ye set up spiritual diseases, cancers, poisons, within the
  body of Him, your great Father,
Who, incorporating mankind, hath sacrificed Himself
To raise you to His own transcendent height
And thus by you He serves is held from further
  progress.
For know that all things, even the mightiest Beings
  advance inevitably toward some higher goal,
Through harmony striving towards perfection.
From atom to god, the Law repeats itself in ever widen-
  ing circles.
Through harmony alone can Nations grow; through
  arts and sciences, through music, through spiritual
  vision ;
Those higher potencies in man which rise ever superior
  to the illusory barriers of race or creed or speech,
As the pure mountain heights serenely stand above the
  confusions of the valley's life.
Only through fuller comprehension and acceptance of
  these immutable laws
Can race combine with race.   For these laws are our very
  essence ;
They are the majestic rhythm of the Thought divine ;
  bright gleams from that ineffable Source which
  flows toward at-one-ment.
Through us, who work as one, its harmonies, the primordial Songs of the creative Sons of Love,
Are ever poured into the minds of those who can contact
  us.
O man, strive then to rend the veil which hides us still ;
Aspire towards perfection, unity of purpose and of
  thought !

Then will all men, all nations, every Race, sounding out
      each his own perfected chord,
Unite in one transcendent symphony.
And we will blaze forth in glory blending our Note with
      yours,
Bringing you bliss and love supernal, drawing you upward
      on mighty chords of sound,
Higher and higher, till the Apex reached,
Perfected man unites with his Great Self
And passes on beyond the Portals
To another Scheme
And to another Dawn.

VIII

THE DIVINE MUSICIAN

I am the harbinger of Love and Peace,
The embodiment of Music,
The perfected rhapsody of fair thoughts and deeds blend-
      ing in unison.
All life is set to music.
By music do the stars spiral together through their
      courses ;
The interplay of every force, from whirl of smallest atom
To that of the Thought issuing forth from out the Night
      of Chaos—
The Song of Vishnu which gives birth to a new Creative
      Day
And rouses the Sons of Action from inertia—
Sounds forth a sacred mantram,
Divine chromatics man cannot hear as yet, alhtough he,
      day and night
Giveth himself forth sound, evil or good, discordant or
      euphonious
According to his nature.
It is from these unceasing tones and overtones
Rising from man's own heart,
Disjunctive waves of broken melody,
Flashes of pure beauty, angry orchestrations of fiendish
      dissonance,
That I, the messenger between man and those great Ones
Who brood over his destiny,
Seek ever to blend, to balance in my mystic scales

And to transmute through my pure heart of love.
I am a ray from the Divine Musician.
When men gather together to perform the great creative
    works
Wherewith we inspire the mighty sons of music on
    the earth,
There in the air above we surge in serried ranks
Building amid the scintillating colours which notes and
    chords give forth
Shapes of transcendent beauty,
Into the heart of which, upon the wings of sound, we
    raise
All those who listen to sublimest heights of rapture ;
And, using this mighty power, radiate love and unity
Upon all the world around.
What once the Priesthood did, that now we do through
    music ;
We are the hierophants of the mysteries,
Seeking to raise through sound man's wandering heart
    to God.
In all the forms which love creates
My attributes are mirrored.
In the clear effulgence which is given forth
By the desire to cherish and protect the weak, the ailing
    and the pitiful,
Whose light is dim or turgid and whose minds whirl in
    discordant cadences of pain ;
In the quiet harmony of peaceful homes ;
In the manifestations of the powers of sex—
That symbol of the universal urge which seeks,
Balancing the pairs of opposites,
In every form, from Planetary Lord to smallest atom,
To blend and merge
The aspects twain into one Perfection—
I manifest my powers of synthesis.
In mother-love—that glowing shaft of rose, that thrill of
    melody—
In any selfless joy ; in children's laughter ;
In every aspect of the love divine which man,

As yet unwittingly, creates ever anew
Within his heart's bright centre, there I work.
I am a part of all quiet, secret joys.
The sweet singing of the small wild bird;
The voice of patient beasts rising from dim fields at
    eventide;
The sibilant whisper of the sun-kissed grass;
The chime of bells across the evening air;
The song of wind and water; all scents and sounds
Chords in nature's mighty pæan of ecstasy
Which riseth night and day throughout the spheres;
All these I blend and use, pouring them down in blessing
Upon whomsoever can respond to me.
Seek then to give, that giving, ye may receive
Ye men, who now toil blindly, weep and strive discord-
    antly;
Open your hearts in love, vibrate to my pure ray,
Search for its emanations.
Then shall ye draw from me such wealth of peace and
    beauty
That your being, o'er filled with bliss, will radiate
    perforce
Its surplus out into that vast reservoir,
The vortex of healing power, wherein all energy is
    garnered
By Those whom I serve, the men divine
Who once were like to you, but now
Stand on the mountain heights
Seeking to draw their brethren to that fount
Of joy to which they have through many weary lives at
    last attained.
They are your Masters; and it is through them,
Adepts indeed of Love,
That perfect symphony is wrought.
It is to them we, luminous spirits, bring these streams of
    sound
This living power which riseth ever from mankind to
    God,
For them to use according to man's need,

Returning the regenerated force again through us, upon
    the earth;
Sounding great chords which rise, expand, outflow,
In forms of power which send an ecstatic thrill through-
    out creation.
Thus, O man, what ye in ignorance have given
That, through the Law of Love, ye receive once again,
    but glorified beyond knowledge.
For whatso'er ye give of good or ill,
Inevitably that will be returned to you.
In this lies your power, your glory—and your woe.
Listen and hear the Law,
The Law which They, your forerunners, have obeyed:
He who dare make the sacrifice for Love,
He who, through Love has suffered and been consumed,
Through Love shall be reborn, and in Love shall find the
    uttermost completion.
Within him shall then be generated the most glorious
    powers
Which only those who sound forth the Note of Unity
Have earned the right to claim:
To bring joy unto the sorrowful;
Hope to those who dwell in the house of weeping;
To bring light to the blind, to open the ears of those who
    are deaf
To the secret melodies of the spheres divine;
To heal those who are sick;
To bring strength to the weak, peace to the afflicted,
    life from the tomb.
Yea, he who could learn to use the mystic Words aright,
To sound the keynote of each living thing,
He would be lord of devas and of men,
Building, disintegrating at his will.
But few there are yet who have unveiled the secret;
Close still is it hid behind adamantine doors.
First must man learn to rule himself,
To sound his own personal note aright,
In harmony with other men and with the Cosmic note
    of Love.

Through training, self-discipline and unremitting service
He cometh to that Door which leads to the Temple
      Courts.
Upon the Door are writ the words: " Love. Serve.
      Obey. Be Silent."
Thence doth the path wind up, toilsome and long.
Yet only to him who follows this path alone
Will be disclosed powers transcendental.
And when at last the greater part of living men
Can wield the secrets and can sound the Notes,
Then once again as in the days of old,
Which we remember, but man hath forgot,
When devas and men together were as gods,
And man could hear and see the supernal rhythms of the
      Cosmic Word
We will combine. And once again
United in love, in concord and in joy
Creation will ring in a celestial flood of melody;
All merging into One
Accomplished harmony.

IX

THE SPIRIT OF LIGHTNING

He who can learn to cup my power within the little
    chalice of his mind,
He who can transmute my elements, my warring attri-
    butes, through his own heart's centre,
Discerning in them th' eternal harmonies of those great
    Cosmic forces
Which oft to men appear destructive,
On him my gifts descend.
Through him my fire shall flow in vitalizing streams,
Into those whirling centres, the Holy Seven,
Wherein are generated his own internal life fires,
Most sacred flames, giving, to him alone who stands
    prepared,
The Powers to make of man a god;
Powers which are mocked at still by those
Who vainly seek to unfold the mysteries of the hidden
    lore
But to abuse them for their own base ends;
So little fitted is man still for knowledge.
Indeed they know me not; nor will they know me yet.
They peer into the dark, blinded by the limitations they,
    in their senseless pride,
Have imposed upon themselves.
But I am there—within them and without.
For I am FOHAT. I am the glow-worm's light; I am the
    fiery furnace.
I the heat man useth for his daily needs; I am the sparks
    unseen

Which animate his being.
I am each aspect of the all-pervasive Flame.
I am the Fire which strikes, destroys, disintegrates,
Purifying the festering plague spots of the earth,
Those centres where, through foolishness of man,
In pestilential streams evil wells up,
With wild, discordant sounds and vaporous loathly forms,
        colours of hell,
Which, when they reach a certain potency—generating
        a force that might, unchecked
Pollute the creative rays ever poured down
To fecundate the earth and raise men's hearts to concord —
Must be destroyed by us, as once Atlantis was,
Through fires, floods and cataclysms.
I am the regenerator.
When inertia falleth, like a blight
Upon mankind, and men grow fat, complacent, during
        some phase
Of material prosperity—good Karma earned in the past
By those who have not yet grown wise enough
To know how best to utilize the good to benefit mankind—
Then do I come like to a cloud of hornets on a summer day
And sting man to activity again,
So that, his body roused from out its slothful ease, his
        mind alert,
He rises up to face his destiny.
Self preservation is the goad which hath from man's
        forgotten past
Pricked him along the thorny path of evolution,
And 'tis this chord I strike in every key, in every octave,
Until at last I sound it, ringing, upon the highest note
Where man seeketh no more to preserve against my fires
His little separate self,
But now defendeth that other self, mankind,
The body of his Logoic Lord.
Yea, he who desireth nothing for himself, who dares
        unite with me his higher mind,
And brave my lightning and my Note which shatters
        him

Whose motive is impure,
To him shall I disclose the secrets of my Power.
In him shall the Serpent raise its fiery head;
The bright wheels shall revolve and he shall see
The atoms whirling in their destined path;
He shall begin to glimpse the pattern and the immensity
      of the Cosmic Plan.
He shall hear an echo of the stupendous harmonies
Through which eternally manifests the Law.
He shall become that Law, the purging fire,—
For I am That.
Then, fused in my lambent heart, he will perceive clear-
      eyed
How we, the mighty agents of the Karmic Lords, strike.
Then shall he know that justice rules, and knowing shall
      feel
Surging within him the same fierce joy that surges through
      our being,
At the command of Law.
Then, working in harmony with us, he shall unite his
      little force
With that stupendous force of which he is a part.
Then shall his small flame leap up, and glow and burn,
Merging once more into that primordial fire which is
      himself and all things.
But he who fears us; he who hath not yet learned
The hidden secrets of our hierarchy,
The union of will with that great purpose which is our
      God;
Or he who hath abused the majesty of Fire,
Let him not seek me out.
He shall be shattered; him shall mine eyes blind.
Beneath the onslaught of my lightning, the thunders of
      my voice,
His quivering nerves and his o'er-chargèd brain shall reel
      and faint
Until he cry, without avail, for peace,
Admitting himself foolish, blind, powerless, before the
      gaze of truth.

Then, knowing, haply, he may turn again and seek
    enlightenment,
Asking to be taught the mysteries of Being,
And find at length that in my hands which slay,
And in my voice which shatters the unworthy, and in
    mine eyes
From which the lightnings strike,
Is Peace for him whose heart is one with All.

SAGITTARIUS

X

THE BUILDERS OF THE NEW AGE

We are the architects of the New Age,
The builders of the coming Race of men,
Inaugurators of the Cyclic change.
Through Us the future speaks;
Through us its Note is sounded forth, its Form is given,
    and its Name made known   .   .   .

Within our centres we become aware of mysteries stirring
Further than our outmost boundaries of contact;
For HE our Lord, Soul of the Sun,
Withdrawn in profoundest meditation beyond all bournes
    of knowledge
Has once again let the great Word go forth.
He and His Brethren,
The Planetary Lords
Have drawn aside another veil.
Their bright regard hath plunged into far realms of
    unrevealēd wisdom
Until this hour unknown by any, save THOSE e'en mightier
    than They.
Now by this act have they become
Initiates in new Powers beyond all ken or thought.
And the dynamic currents from Their supernal minds,
Re-charged by this stupendous evolution,
Rush forth, stimulating every cell
Within the worlds which are Their bodies.
From some far secret Solar System
At the reverberations of the great Note,

A new Rod of Power is generated.
Magnetic waves, strange, mighty, fraught with potentiali-
    ties
As yet undreamed-of on the lower planes,
Are straight released, radiating through interplanetary
    space,
And Form responds upon the Seven Planes.
Those Who Know
Sound forth the tonal harmonies, ope wide the door
Through which the liberated forces flow
Towards the Earth—their focus.
Then do we stir,
Archers of Heaven,
Lords of the Coming Age,
Sons of Primordial Fire,
Warriors of light, we speed
With Devic hosts to do our bidding ;
Enlisting in our ranks beings from every Kingdom :
The powers of Heat and Air, spirits of Water, Builders of
    Form,
And They who guide the Nations and who weave the
    harmonies of the Spheres.
The old magnetic currents which have stimulated the
    earth
For ages past, in rhythmic harmony,
Resist our invading Force,
But are thrown from their rotating centres.
Long will it be ere they can coalesce
And balance be achieved.
Conflict in Heaven !
Conflict upon the Earth !
The ancient Note splits into discord.
All things become aware of the great change.
Man in his triple world is shaken.
Instinctively he repulses the regenerating force.
In throes of travail his wild cry goes up ;
Blindly within himself he senses now
The pitiless work of dissolution and re-birth.
In frantic fear he clings to safety, to the magic formulae

With which for ages he hath wrought and built and lived ;
The old ideas die slow, in agony ;
They writhe their way back into reiterations of outworn
     forms,
They seek to keep what they have won.
It is forbidden.
Man prays in his bewilderment to the gods he hath long
     since discarded ;
He struggles, seeing around him nought but catastrophe.
Beneath his feet the solid-seeming earth rocks ;
On every side stalk dreadful phantoms.
The weaklings go down, perish beneath the onslaught
Of these new forces which they cannot co-relate.
They pass and are no more seen.
But some—the few,
Fathers of the new Race, respond.
Fearless and bold, from eager feet they shake
The dust of old dreams aside ;
Seekers for Truth in every age, unswervingly
They bare their bodies to our mystic shafts ;
Loudly they demand that light be given
And that Truth be shown.
Then, only then, can my great voice be heard ;
Then, only then, can I reveal my form—
Pattern to which the new man must aspire.
Uplifted on the pinions of the new dawn I stand,
     cleaving the mists of ignorance,
Holding up the glass wherein is mirrored,
For him who dares to gaze into its dread depths,
The mystery of that which is to be.

     .   .   .   .

O man, my brother, thou who dost desire to work with me ;
O man, who knewest me not until within thy heart,
Urged by the voice of thy Lord, thou didst sound forth
     my note,
I greet thee !
Strange will my paths be to thee, stranger will be my
     language ;

Yet if thou dost seek to learn of me,
If thou wilt be to men my true interpreter,
Thou must be willing to be separated from among thy
      brethren
Who are not ready yet to hear my voice which would
      but cause confusion
To them from whom discord and error rise up perpet-
      ually.
Yet do thou too beware, my son ; for it will shatter thee,
Unless thy whole being is attuned to my great note.
Be warned then, seek me not out, unless thou, O fore-
      runner,
O bold searcher, art willing to pass through the portals of
      Flame ;
To receive initiation into the Mysteries of the New Age ;
To enter the hazardous realms of the Devas
Who work isolated from man's emanations ;
And thence to return a brand for the burning,
A scapegoat, the sacrifice for those who, behind thee,
Blinded by truth, will turn and will rend thee.
But if thou be courageous, armed with love and com-
      passion,
If still thou desirest to work with me and my brothers,
Then lift thy mind above the confusions of the earth ;
Gaze clear-eyed upon truth.   Fear nothing ! In struggle,
      in defeat,
Aye, even in death, is strength added to strength.
Through knowledge shall thy mind become lucid and
      stable ;
Thou shalt KNOW and for ever be freed from all doubting.
Then will I guide thee through the caves of Emotion, the
      tides of Desire, into the fires of my being.
I will change and transmute thee, that in thy mind, as
      in those of thy fellows—
The seers, the creators—the events of the future shall be
      faintly reflected.
For know, O my child, that the time now approacheth
When in man's form among you will come for your
      guidance,

The harbingers of the new age.
Ancient wrongs must be righted, the balance adjusted.
Not for man alone shineth the new dawn.
The sons of the Third[1] shall rejoice with their masters.
To them also cometh an Avatar, a redeemer.
He, Lord of the beasts, will teach man to repay
The debt that he oweth to his little brothers
Whom still he doth slay for greed or for wanton sport,
Breaking the laws divine, destroying that harmony,
    which is goal of Creation.
Herein lies the schism ; this is the curse on man
Who was given, in ancient times, lordship over the earth,
    the three lower kingdoms.
For upon him the charge was laid to shield and to guide
All forms of that life—whose forms once were his own—
And lead them upward along the ascending arc of evolu-
    tion.
That charge he doth betray with every act of suffering
    he doth cause,
E'en though, in selfish blindness, he may persuade him-
    self the act be justified ;
Thus hath he brought the judgment on himself that he,
    by causing confusion in the lower worlds,
By using his great power for basest ends, cannot himself
    find peace
Until he hath repaid these ancient debts.
The New Race will be shown by Him who cometh the path
    of regeneration.
And, quickened by these new waves of planetary force
    which even now
Are playing upon the earth, man will evolve the powers
    to perceive
The inner truth, to read the souls of animals and men,
To enter, through the magic of sympathy and love all
    kingdoms
Higher and lower than his own.
Devas will be his teachers. His eye of light shall be
    unclosed

[1] Animal Kingdom.

And he will see then into fair realms he now derideth.
Then shall he be taught the powers of speech.   He shall
    address
Devas and gods in their own parlance.
His Kings and Statesmen then will be Initiates
And will contact the great Adepts for guidance in the
    affairs of man.
Thus will the race, through centuries of striving, rise
    toward a still more glorious stage ;
Illumination will pour once more from on high.
In that far day the more advanced of that Sixth Race of
    men,
Will have transmuted sex, conquered emotion and burned
    out all transitory desire ;
This high aim accomplished, then
Will they be taught to use the powers of mind to build
    the bodies of their children ;
And to combine in these most glorious beings, the finer
    qualities of either sex :
Purified love, intuition, powerful, one-pointed will,
Wisdom, activity—the secrets of creation, so that they
    in their turn, may build in sound, colour and
    form.
Long must ye wait for this.
Yet even now, for him who hath eyes to see, the first
    faint signs
Of this far, promised day are manifest, for already
The beneficent gods draw mankind towards their goal.
Into the minds of those whose imaginations, winged by
    burning desire
To help the world, uplift them for one ecstatic instant
    into the realm of Ideation
Where time is not and the end can be perceived,
Transient flashes from this bright dawn are cast ;
Into their hands is given the torch lit by this flame divine,
    this rising sun of glory.
It is for them, whom with my burning arrow I have sealed
    to be my messengers,
To guide man's faltering steps toward this light.

It is for them, forerunners of the new age, whose eyes
      have looked into mine own,
Whose ears have heard my voice, to launch their brethren
      forth upon the great, surging tides of evolution;
To be their pilot and their guiding star, drawing them
      ever upward towards the sacred heights,
The Holy Mountain, birth-place of the Race to be,
Where Man, his eyes opened, shall at last behold himself
Transfigured, glorified,
Himself no more
But merged and one with All.

CAPRICORN

XI

THE GUARDIAN OF THE HEIGHTS

I am the Spirit of the Mountains,
The symbolic form of life in every stage.
From the dull earth—the body—I arise
To water, restless and illusory like man's desires ;
Thence my seams soar upward to those pure heights
      serene
Where nought stirs but the great wind of Spirit
Sweeping over icy snows ; where the rays from our Lord
      the Sun
Pour down unchecked by atmospheric veils.
I am the sacred Mount,
The unfolding Lotus ;
The dense body of that Holy One,
Soul of the Earth—the Silent Watcher.
In me are combined all elements and kingdoms ;
In me all potentialities unite from lowest to highest.
My feet are set deep in the Central Fires ;
Deep in the secret place where the great Snake is curled,
Where gaseous elements unite to transmute the eternally
      whirling atoms,
Where stability taketh its final dense, illusory form.
Here spirit burns and crystallizes into the treasures of the
      mineral world :
Rubies and emeralds ; diamonds, the emblem of Will
      and Knowledge ;
And gold that hath the power to set men's passions
      flaming with greed.

Molten processes, chemical changes that the scientists—
    e'en alchemists of old—
Imagined not, are here created by infinite, swarming
    forms of life :
Gnomes, salamanders, dark elemental shapes, mindless
    instinctive beings,
Etheric giants and pigmies, who know not light of sun,
    or breath of air.
Tremendous forces stir in my dark depths, servants of
    the great Law.
Sometimes, propelled by mysterious cosmic changes, or
    invoked
By mankind's own destructive emanations,
The Terrible Ones, who dwell within the vortices of earth's
    profoundest caverns
Are roused from their dread sleep, and rending their
    prison house
Arise with glaring eyes and pinions dark into the upper
    air.
Then the rocks crack, th' internal fires belch forth ;
All life within the bounds of their jurisdiction is straight
    extinguished,
Continents are sunk and oceans churn.
The spirits of the blue magnetic fires, the Great Regener-
    ators,
Shiva's mighty sons, leap to the call.
Destroyers and creators both, they cleanse the planet,
    building it anew
With fresh combinings of our elements to serve its needs.
We are the bony structure of the world, its mighty back-
    bone, nerves and arteries
Through which the sacred forces flow which give it life
    and health
And feed the myriad beings who take from it their
    substance.
We it is, the tall mountain gods, who draw from all our
    planes
The living forces up to that high peak where air and ether
    meet,

Transmuting them into spiritual qualities in higher
    spheres beyond the ken of man.
From out our secret centres well the springs, life-blood
    of the earth,
To feed the rivers which flow down to irrigate the vine-
    yards and the fields,
Spreading our benediction over the plains and cities
Where pullulate the restless sons of men, the voice of
    whose discontent
Riseth like to the buzz of wasps into our peaceful dwelling
    place.
We ever seek to entice men hither, that they may
    repose
Their weary bodies on our vernal breast, and find the
    peace
That only we can give, wrapped in the calm of wis-
    dom.
From out our heart healing we pour into their veins
    poisoned
By the exhalations of their world ; we cleanse them with
    our living breath.
Bathed in the aura of our love, wrapped in our silence
Where there is nothing to distract the mind, the soul
    can speak,
And thought and aspiration can give birth unto their
    most holy powers.
For know O man, O seeker, that upon these our heights
When thou hast risen so far, and shaken off the fetters
    which bind thee still to denser earth,
To the affections of the destructive fires of passion,
To the flowing waters of thine own desires,
There shalt thou find the Holy Ones
Those who, having trod the paths of life and learned
    all it can teach,
Have earned the right to keep themselves apart working
    from afar,
Detached and calm, undeafened by the restless noise
    of voices, passions, fears ;
Unconfused by the illusory images of Time.

They are the embodied mind, the visible aspect of the
    Logos' Will;
They form the mighty Brotherhood of Love, Chohans,
    Adepts, Masters,
Leaders unrecognized of the multitudinous activities of
    lesser men,
Firstfruits of perfected humanity—the mirror wherein
    man may glimpse himself as he must yet become.
They live on earth, although ye know them not, and
    sceptic mock,
And Western knowledge fail to understand their work
    or find their hidden dwellings.
Where else should be those Avatars of old, the seers, the
    men of genius,
The mighty Thinkers who taught you wisdom and were
    to their lesser fellows as men to ants?
Those who brought down for you the torch of Truth to
    illuminate your shadow-haunted way,
Think ye that they were swept into some Limbo, to some
    unknown star?
Not so. Love, for which they did strive and live and
    die, bindeth them to you still;
Will bind them till the last man has become one of them,
    reached bliss and liberation.
This is a part of that mysterious Sacrifice of which all
    Holy Books throughout the ages tell:
The sacrifice of those who, of their own free will, refused
    bliss beyond thinking
To remain with you, protect and guide you until the very
    end
When they will be freed through your achievement.
But for ages past while man, rejecting their teaching,
    mocking their wisdom,
Casting them forth with indifference or hate,
Sank slowly into the darkness of the Age of Iron,
They had perforce, to dwell apart, hidden within my
    fastnesses of ice and snow,
Protected by my guardians of wind and water,
My rushing torrents and my rocky heights,

Only descending into the haunts of men when, by no
     other means,
Could fresh stimulus and enlightenment be given.
But now at last man's ardent cry for truth, rising from
     every side in streams of power
Hath merited a new response.
Already, a little, hath the veil been lifted.
Using the devas as their instruments and intermediaries,
They have poured down fresh inspiration to enlighten
     the more receptive among the sons of men ;
Conscious, living particles of the Mind of the Planetary
     Lord,
Seeing all as one, the Past, the Present and that which the
     Present shall become,
Aware, through their own experience, of man's utmost
     need,
They only can give humanity the bread and wine its
     starving soul desires.
To the few, their pupils,
Those forerunners who have dared to force their way
     towards the icy heights of wisdom,
Men chosen by them and trained in divers way ;
Men who have been tested and proved faithful, who,
     out of the surrounding dark
Have let their light shine forth,
To these have the Masters ever revealed themselves.
And throughout the ages ever in secrecy have poured
     their wisdom down.
But now in this age of change, more light will be vouch-
     safed,
That by its gleams the path spiralling the mountain side
     can be perceived by all.
Now into the minds of those who have learned to answer
     to the vibration
Of Love without Desire which the Adepts give forth ;
Who freely can breathe the thin airs of this pure mental
     plane ;
Who, fearless and strong, will leap the chasm,
Brave the sharp rocks, and like the mountain goat,

Symbol of those who fear no height nor depth,
Climb with sure feet the perilous ways towards the
    dizzy peaks,
Into the heart of these shall power and knowledge flow.
Already, although they realize it not, many are being led
    from plains and cities,
Through jungles, deserts, through waters perilous,
    towards my brooding peaks.
Aye, they will be so led until the end ; they will be lifted
    by the strong hands of love,
Towards the sacred heights of Meru, the Holy Mountain,
Into the very heart of the pure Lotus,
Where they will become
One with the Thought Divine,
One with their God,
The Absolute Existence, Knowledge, Bliss.

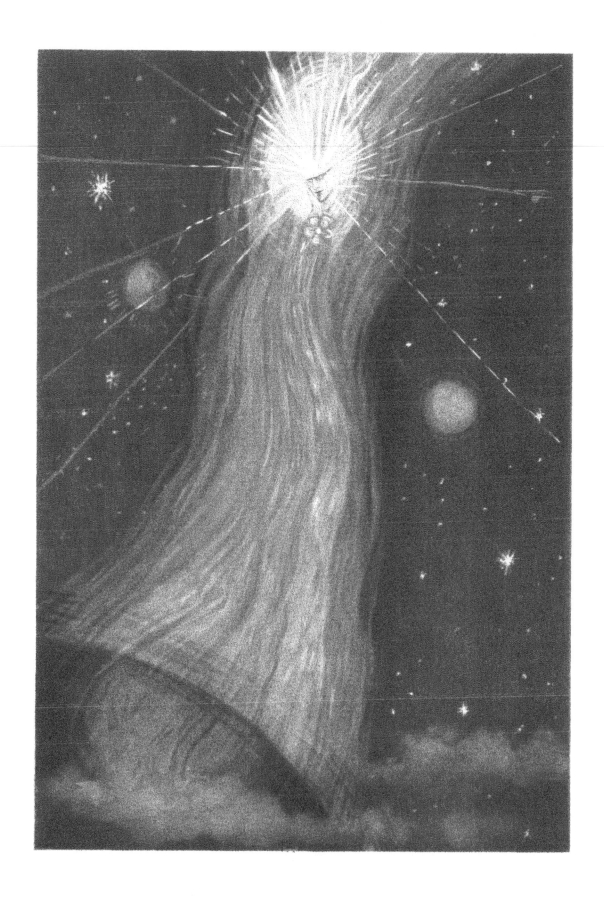

AQUARIUS

XII

THE COSMIC MESSENGERS

From interplanetary Space,
From realms beyond the range of finite thought,
Where Time is not and darkness blends with light in
    THAT for which there is no sign or name,
The primordial Sons of Creative Fire project Their will,
Evolving and disintegrating Form throughout the Seven
    Planes,
And through us, their swift messengers, and all our
    lesser brethren,
Even to that being which ensouls the whirling atom,
Guide and direct the currents, vibrations, waves of what-
    ever type of force the Plan requires ;
Balancing evil and good, darkness and light, in the great
    scales of perfect equilibrium.
For Action and Reaction are the manifestation of the
    Cosmic Law,
And only man blinded by his senses, thinking the Part
    the Whole,
Sees Good and Evil eternally separate—knowing not that
    all is one,
For whene'er a vortex hath been formed of creative
    energies
A void remains when these are exhausted or withdrawn—
Perfect is the Law, evolving all things towards adjust-
    ment ;
Each thing is a facet of the whole ;
A myriad particles of fiery life, Fohat's mysterious sons,

Are set in swift rotation by the faintest breath;
No sound, no thought, no movement in any centre of
    manifesting life,
But createth a ripple which floweth throughout all realms
    of being
To distances so vast man's comprehension reels before
    such possibilities.
In all creation life responds to life.
Each centre of the indwelling life draws to itself by its
    own mysterious individual magnetism
What it doth need for its expansion.
As the mighty forces sweep in cyclic pulsations, dynamic
    energies,
Upon man's little world, uniting all in the One,
So doth the microcosm of man's body respond; each of
    his atoms
Recognizing unfailingly in the majestic choir, its parent
    note.
From stars, from planets, from energy generated
Within the mysterious centres of the Zodiacal Signs,
Man draws his substance; gathering in the particles he
    needs,
Building throughout his life by act and thought,
    spiritual atoms
Which, after his death, will latent lie until he calls them
    forth to re-incarnate in him,
That he may reap what he hath sown.
And in like manner doth every living thing
Reflect the impress of planetary powers,
Transmutes them or receives from them the fatal impulse
    of its doom.
There is no separate existence; the same Breath
    vitalizes
Even those Nameless Ones into Whose minds the Creator
    reflects His will;
For e'en the greatest must receive and must transmute
    mysterious forces
According to the same Law as Man in the development of
    the rhythm

To which all things from the dull earth clod to the
    remotest star
Eternally evolve.
This Law is the Universal Key.
They, Beings of awe-ful magnitude, guard for you the doors
To that dread mystery, the Ring-Pass-Not, whence
    powers from the Unknown
Will, at the appointed hour, flow in upon your world.
Aye, the dread change draws near !
Another Race, sons of Aquarius,
Seek even now to fashion themselves a dwelling-place
    upon the earth,
And for their work new powers are requisite ;
The sacred Doors are opened
And we, Spirits of the far realms of space,
Are bidden now pour. forth this new life in Cosmic
    rays as yet unknown to man
And bring to him the message of the Spheres,
Revealing mysteries until now shrouded and concealed.
Through us shall man be given the sacred Words ;
Through us, who stand upon the whirling circles of the
    Seven Spheres,
Who watch ever for the Sign ; wait for the sacred Word ;
Who live to create according to the Will of THAT which
    made us,
Will sound forth the call to man to watch and wait and
    serve with us.
But each man hath freewill ; he may refuse to work
    toward perfection ;
He may choose to breast the current ; to endeavour
    to stem the tides of God ;
He may oppose his puny will to the great will of love
    which urgeth him ever
Toward that union wherein alone he will find the con-
    summation of all his visions, all his aspirations ;
He may fight on, blinded by his dream of separateness ;
Knowing not That which he is ;
Warring against phantom hosts—his own delusions ;
Beating his fists against the dank walls of the prison house

Which he himself hath builded, when upon his right
hand,
The door to liberation standeth wide.
The God within will wait ; He knoweth Himself inde-
structible ;
When the man turneth toward the light, He will be there
to lead him forth.
Aye, when man desires at last to unite with the divine
will,
To play his part aright in the stupendous symphony of
Cosmic Ideation ;
When he would learn the secrets of the stars, the ebb and
flow
Of planetary waves which, like the sea, dissolve all things
into their elements ;
When he would know how he can rule his own destiny
through perfect comprehension
Of the great Law of Karma, and learn to vibrate alone
to the highest octave,
Where all conflicting elements blend in one harmony ;
When he desires to see and comprehend the infinitely
small, the infinitely great,
And how he himself may balance these two extremes
between which he now hangeth helplessly,
Caught within the web of his own ignorance ;
When he would learn to use the elements, drawing on
powers which in him latent lie,
And without which the scientist will seek for Truth in
vain ;
Then he must turn to Them Who Know ; and putting
his pride of intellect,
His personal desires, his blind allegiance to instruments
of finite sense humbly by,
Ask that he be shown the way to higher wisdom ; that
he be trained and disciplined anew ;
That all his faculties be enlightened so that he may
glimpse truth,
No longer with the vision of fallible human mind but with
the clear sight of Eternity.

But only through seeking out the Ancient Way, wherein
the sages of the world have trod,
Can man hope to regain the knowledge and the power
which he,
Through abuse in ancient, forgotten days did forfeit ;
When because of his pride and destructive might, the
Word went forth
And out the fair garden where with us, Powers of the
Elements, he wrought,
Wielding our mighty forces, hearing the great harmonies of
colour and of sound,
Passing at will into the higher spheres of intuitional
perception,
He was driven into bitter exile, into the dark of the
limitations of that ignorance
Wherein still he wanders, blind and dumb, lost in the
mists of separateness.
Only when he hath controlled every emotion and
harnessed his personal will,
Only when it hath become impossible to him ever to use
our powers destructively,
When through selfless love alone doth he desire to lift the
veil from Truth,
And like unto us evermore strive, work, exist alone
According to the Will of the One Lord of Life,
Can he be re-united consciously to that Son of Light
which is himself.
Then will the final veil be torn aside,
Then will he behold the supernal glory of what he is,
Not darkly any more—but face to face ;
The which beholding, he will himself become
The Light, the Life, the Truth, the Way.